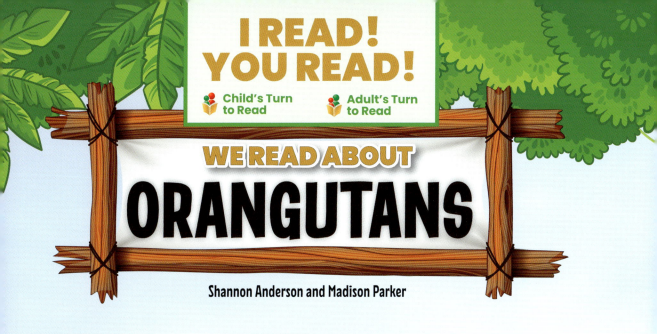

Shannon Anderson and Madison Parker

Table of Contents

ORANGUTANS	3
WORDS TO KNOW	22
INDEX	23
COMPREHENSION QUESTIONS	23

Parent and Caregiver Guide

Reading aloud with your child has many benefits. It expands vocabulary, sparks discussion, and promotes an emotional bond. Research shows that children who have books read aloud to them have improved language skills, leading to greater school success.

I Read! You Read! books offer a fun and easy way to read with your child. Follow these guidelines.

Before Reading

- Look at the front and back covers. Discuss personal experiences that relate to the topic.
- Read the *Words to Know* at the back of the book. Talk about what the words mean.
- If the book will be challenging or unfamiliar to your child, read it aloud by yourself the first time. Then, invite your child to participate in a second reading.

During Reading

 Have your child read the words beside this symbol. This text has been carefully matched to the reading and grade levels shown on the cover.

 You read the words beside this symbol.

- Stop often to discuss what you are reading and to make sure your child understands.
- If your child struggles with decoding a word, help them sound it out. If it is still a challenge, say the word for your child and have them repeat it after you.
- To find the meaning of a word, look for clues in the surrounding words and pictures.

After Reading

- Praise your child's efforts. Notice how they have grown as a reader.
- Use the *Comprehension Questions* at the back of the book.
- Discuss what your child learned and what they liked or didn't like about the book.

Most importantly, let your child know that reading is fun and worthwhile. Keep reading together as your child's skills and confidence grow.

ORANGUTANS

A zoo is a fun place to see animals and learn about them.

One animal you may find in a zoo is an orangutan.

CHILD

A zoo is a type of park where many kinds of animals live. Zoos help protect the animals inside them.

ADULT

Orangutans are the largest animals that live in trees.

They are **primates**.

They belong to the ape family.

Orangutans have opposable thumbs they can use to hold objects.

Humans are primates, too. That means we are related to orangutans!

Orangutans have red hair.

Their arms are longer than their legs.

They are very good at climbing and moving around in trees.

When an orangutan spreads its arms wide, the distance from one fingertip to the other fingertip is over seven feet (two meters) long!

An orangutan's favorite food is fruit.

Orangutans also eat seeds, bark, and sometimes insects.

Orangutans are omnivores. Omnivores eat both plants and animals. Humans are omnivores, too.

Orangutans mostly like to live alone.

But orangutan moms stay with their babies and care for them for many years.

Living alone helps an orangutan find enough food. There may not be enough food in one area for a whole group.

An orangutan baby is called a "baby," just like humans.

Orangutans are **mammals**, so babies drink their mom's milk.

A **mammal** is a type of animal. Mammals are vertebrates, which means they have a backbone. They also have hair or fur.

The mom carries her baby around with her.

She teaches her baby how to find food and build a nest for sleeping.

Orangutan babies live with their moms for six or seven years. They learn all they need to know for living in the wild.

Orangutans are smart.

They use sticks as tools to help them get and eat food.

Like all apes, orangutans are intelligent. Just like humans, orangutans use tools. Sticks help them get seeds from fruit and insects from inside holes in trees.

Orangutans teach each other to use tools.

Orangutans make noises and move their bodies to **communicate**.

Some of their sounds are barks, squeaks, and screams.

When they are annoyed, orangutans make a high-pitched sound. They can also make a raspberry-like noise when they stick their tongue between their lips and blow.

Some orangutans have learned sign language from humans.

Orangutans live in **rainforests** on two islands in **Asia**.

If you cannot go to Asia to see orangutans, you can find them at the zoo!

Even though **rainforests** cover a small part of Earth, many animals live there. Out of every ten animal species, eight live in the rainforest.

Words to Know

Asia (AY-zhuh): one of Earth's continents; a very large landmass in Earth's eastern hemisphere north of the equator

communicate (kuh-MYOO-ni-kate): to share information, feelings, or ideas with others

mammals (MAM-uhlz): animals that have hair or fur, that give birth to live babies, and that make milk to feed their babies

primates (PRYE-mates): members of the group of mammals that includes monkeys, apes, and people

rainforests (RAYN-for-ists): forests in tropical regions of the world where it rains a lot

Index

Asia 20, 21
baby/babies 11, 12, 14
food 8, 11, 14, 16
sounds 18
tools 16, 17
trees 4, 7, 16

Comprehension Questions

1. What kind of mammal is an orangutan?
    a. a marsupial   b. a rodent   c. a primate

2. What do orangutans like to eat the most?
    a. fruit   b. frogs   c. snakes

3. Baby orangutans are called ___.
    a. babies   b. cubs   c. monkeys

4. True or False: Orangutans like to live in big groups.

5. True or False: Orangutans are good at moving around in caves.

Answers
1. c 2. a 3. a 4. False 5. False

Written by: Shannon Anderson and Madison Parker
Design by: Under the Oaks Media
Editor: Kim Thompson

Library of Congress PCN Data
We Read About Orangutans / Shannon Anderson and Madison Parker
I Read! You Read!
ISBN 979-8-8873-5305-0 (hard cover)
ISBN 979-8-8873-5390-6 (paperback)
ISBN 979-8-8873-5475-0 (EPUB)
ISBN 979-8-8873-5560-3 (eBook)
Library of Congress Control Number: 2023930214

Printed in the United States of America.

Photographs/Shutterstock: Gudkov Andrey: cover;
Don Mammoser: p. 3; Asia Travel: p. 5; Stephen Lavery:
p. 6; Kylie Nicholson: p. 9; Katesalin Pagkaihang:
p. 10; Capatin AI: p. 12; Sergio Bertino: p. 13;
lukaZemanphoto: p. 14; Ricky Santana: p. 15

Seahorse Publishing Company
www.seahorsepub.com

Copyright © 2024 **SEAHORSE PUBLISHING COMPANY**

All rights reserved. No part of this publication may be reproduced, stored in a retrieval system or be transmitted in any form or by any means, electronic, mechanical, photocopying, recording, or otherwise, without the prior written permission of Seahorse Publishing Company.

Published in the United States
Seahorse Publishing
PO Box 771325
Coral Springs, FL 33077